BUSES:
OLD TECHNOLOGY
REFINED

KEITH A. JENKINSON

AMBERLEY

First published 2024

Amberley Publishing
The Hill, Stroud
Gloucestershire, GL5 4EP

www.amberley-books.com

ISBN 978 1 3981 2213 0 (print)
ISBN 978 1 3981 2214 7 (ebook)

British Library Cataloguing in Publication Data.
A catalogue record for this book is available from
the British Library.

Origination by Amberley Publishing.
Printed in the UK.

Introduction

Like many things in life, 'what goes around comes around' and this can be clearly seen in public road transport, especially in the different forms of propulsion. First, of course, was the horse-drawn era, and then followed various forms of mechanical development with the use of steam, electricity, battery, gas, petrol, diesel and then hydrogen all making an appearance. During the latter part of the twentieth century, global warming and growing environmental concerns caused a move away from fossil fuels towards non-polluting sources of power, bringing electricity and battery propulsion back into the equation, and with government support and an upcoming ban on the production of petrol- and diesel-engined vehicles in 2030 and hybrid vehicles in 2035, these are said to be the future of private and public transport.

While this book is not intended to be a definitive history of the evolution of public road transport, it has been necessary to briefly look back at how it all began in the seventeenth century and how it has been developed over the years through different fuels and vehicle design, etc., and how in a number of cases today's transport is merely a refined and developed repeat of the past, proving that nothing is totally new.

Without the help of many others who have generously allowed me to use their photographs, it would not have been possible to illustrate all the developments that have taken place over four centuries, and to them I say a massive 'thank you'. Where known, all these people have been credited at the end of the photo captions, but unfortunately it has not been possible to identify a few, and to those I offer my sincere apologies and have shown them as 'author's collection'.

Old Technology Refined

From an age where little or no consideration was given to the environment to the current growing concern about global warming, public transport, along with everything else in life, has undergone a steady change through experiments, progress and new technology, and will undoubtedly continue to do so in the years ahead. However, in order to move forward, we must look back at the developments made by our forefathers to see the progress that has been achieved.

Despite the recent hype relating to gas-fuelled buses and battery-electric passenger-carrying vehicles, it should be remembered that in the UK, as too in various overseas countries, these concepts have been around for over a hundred years. But before all this there were several other means of public road vehicle propulsion, starting with the horse-drawn era.

Public road transport reportedly began in 1610 when the first recorded stagecoach service was inaugurated from Edinburgh to Leith, and as the seventeenth century progressed, so did the stagecoach, which began to operate on longer routes, some of which spanned the length of the UK, took several days to complete and used staging inns along the way for overnight stops. As coach designs and road improvements were made, travel by stagecoach steadily gained in popularity with more and more services being started, all of which needed to be pre-booked, and it was not until the development of the railways and canals in the mid-1800s that they began to decline and ultimately vanish.

A well-loaded stagecoach pulled by four horses. (Author's collection)

There was, however, still the need for public transport in areas before railways reached them, particularly in larger towns and cities, and to fill this, horse-drawn public transport made its appearance across the UK. Although first seen in France, the horse bus ultimately made its debut in Britain in 1824 when John Greenwood began a service in Manchester which required no prior booking and drivers could pick up or set down passengers anywhere upon request. Seeing the success of this new mode of city transport, on 4 July 1829 thirty-two-year-old coachbuilder George Shillibeer inaugurated a service in London from Paddington to Bank, a move which prompted others to enter the fray.

As the market developed, in 1850 Thomas Tilling joined the growing ranks of horse bus operators, followed in 1855 by the newly founded London General Omnibus Company. Throughout the remaining years of the nineteenth century, horse buses were to be seen in large numbers in London and also in cities across the UK, albeit in lesser quantities, but from around 1890 they began to be replaced by tramways and in the early 1900s by motor buses. However, it was not until 4 August 1914 that the last examples ran on the streets of London when Thomas Tilling removed them from its route between Peckham and Honor Oak.

Prior to this, the first horse trams appeared in 1807 when Swansea & Mumbles Railway opened a service between Swansea and Oystermouth. Whether this was a tramway or railway is open to debate, but despite having been opened as freight railway a year earlier, it was the first operation on metal rails to carry passengers. It was not until 30 August 1860, however, that the first 'proper' street tramway was opened when Birkenhead Street Railway Company began a service from Birkenhead Park to Woodside Ferry on 5-foot 2-inch-gauge track. Following this, horse trams made their appearance in several other towns and cities across the UK, and although most of these were subsequently converted to electric traction, the final examples were not withdrawn until 6 October 1926 (in Morecambe), although they are still operational today during summer months in Douglas, Isle of Man.

Shillibeer's first horse-drawn bus, dating from 1829. (Author's collection)

Typifying the horse bus is this London General Omnibus Co. example, seen here after being preserved. (Author's collection)

Pictured in a London suburb is this well-loaded four-horse double-deck bus operated by Thomas Tilling. (Author's collection)

Seen in the early to mid-1800s well laden with passengers and goods is this Swansea & Mumbles Railway double-deck horse-drawn tram. (Author's collection)

Two Morecambe Corporation horse-drawn trams make their way along the resort's promenade in the early 1920s. (Author's collection)

The world's oldest horse trams in the northern hemisphere still operate today in Douglas, Isle of man, where toast rack car 48 is seen here hauled, as always, by a single horse. (Author's collection)

Following these, other forms of tramway propulsion arrived using steam, cable, and town gas. Although steam trams – which were steam locomotives hauling unpowered trams – first appeared in Leeds and Bristol in 1880, they were mainly operated in the Midlands and the north of England. To eliminate excessive smoke, the government ruled that it was illegal to fire them with coal, and that instead coke had to be used. Although they had largely been replaced by the turn of the century, those operated by Rossendale Valley Tramways lasted until July 1909 while those on the Grimsby & Immingham Railway survived until May 1921 and the last of all were on the Swansea & Mumbles Railway where they surprisingly continued in operation until 1929. Meanwhile, cable-hauled trams were only to be seen in London and Edinburgh, with the former opening a line from Archway to Highgate Village on 28 May 1884, and from Brixton Hill to Streatham in 1891, these closing in 1909 and 1904 respectively. Edinburgh's first cable tramway opened on 26 January 1888 and was joined by a second route in 1890, both of which remained in operation until June 1923. Following these, a third cable tramway was opened, in Llandudno in 1902. Although ascending the Great Orme, it can more likely be seen as a mountain tramway and is still in operation today.

Of greater rarity, and only appearing in two towns in the UK, were trams powered by town gas. These were introduced by Lytham St Annes Corporation in July 1896, and after their withdrawal in 1903 some of them were sold for further service to Neath Corporation in South Wales where they continued in use until August 1920.

After all these, another form of public road transport appeared in the UK in 1883 when some operators began turning their attention to paraffin-fired steam-driven buses, the design of which, when first appearing in 1833, resembled stagecoaches without horses. Somewhat short-lived, they disappeared from the scene until 1898, when fitted with what later became more traditional bus bodywork, and built by Clarkston, Chelmsford, they were reintroduced to a few towns and cities across the UK. Although never gaining a great deal of popularity, the last examples to remain in service survived until 1923, operating in Torquay. Following this, for haulage work some manufacturers such as Mann, Garrett, Foden and Sentinel began building steam wagons which had been developed from coal-fired traction engines and the latter remarkably continued their production until as late as 1938.

Hauling a four-wheel double-deck tramcar at Stamford Hill, London, *c.* 1885 is this steam tram locomotive. (Author's collection)

Illustrated here is a Rossendale Valley Tramways Company's steam tram near Rawtenstall, *c.* 1900. (Commercial postcard)

Two Metropolitan Street Tramways cable-hauled trams pass each other on Brixton Hill in 1891. (Author's collection)

Pictured in 2018 are two trams at a passing loop on the cable-operated Great Orme mountain tramway, Llandudno. (Author's collection)

Seen in the early 1900s is Neath Corporation Tramways gas tram 21 en route to Briton Ferry. (Author's collection)

Seen in London in 1913 operated by National Steam Car Co., this was an open-top steam-driven double-decker built by Thomas Clarkson, Chelmsford. (Author's collection)

Another Clarkson open-top double-deck steam bus. C5519 was owned by Harrogate Road Car Co. and is seen here filling with water from a pipe on the pavement at Starbeck terminus *c.* 1911. (Author's collection)

Meanwhile, also in 1883, the first electric trams made their debut when they were launched on a 1.24-mile route along Brighton's seafront by Volk's Electric Tramway, and as the oldest in the world, it still operates in 2024. While most of the forthcoming electric tramways used overhead wires for their power supply, a few adopted the conduit system with power being gained from an underground rail accessed through a slot between the running tracks, with London particularly favouring this.

Over the following years, electric trams powered largely by municipally owned electricity companies replaced the earlier forms of public road transport in numerous towns and cities the length and breadth of the UK, and although some had comparatively short lives before being replaced by buses or trolleybuses, a number survived, mainly as a result of the Second World War, through the 1940s and 1950s, and it was not until 31 August 1962 that the final examples (except for those in Blackpool and the Isle of Man, which are still operating today) passed into history after their withdrawal in Glasgow. Some thirty years later, however, trams made a reappearance on the streets of Manchester, followed by Sheffield, Croydon, Birmingham, Wolverhampton, Nottingham and Edinburgh.

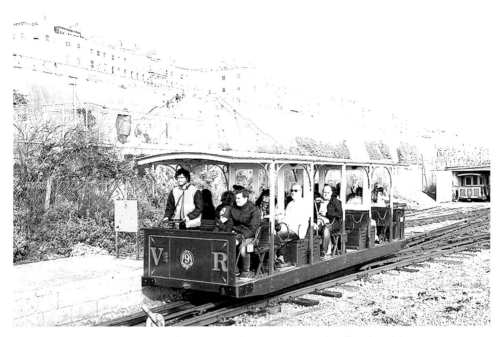

Still operating today on the seafront at Brighton is a tram of Volks, the oldest narrow-gauge electric tramway in the world, which began operation in 1883. (Author's collection)

Seen on the conduit track on Victoria Embankment during their final week of operation in July 1952 are two London Transport HR2 class trams. (Author's collection)

Bradford Corporation Transport's electric trams remained in operation until 1950 and never had covered upper-deck balconies, thus giving them a truly antique appearance. Here 102 heads to Odsal on the service from the city centre during the final months of its life. (Author's collection)

Leeds Corporation Tramways Chamberlain tram 69 stands at Gipton terminus still wearing its pre-1950 dark blue livery. (Author's collection)

Manx Electric Railway electric-powered car 21 is seen here hauling a toast rack trailer at the Derby Castle terminus, Douglas, on 31 May 1973. Both trams still operate today. (K. A. Jenkinson)

The first UK city to reintroduce electric trams in the last decade of the twenty-first century was Manchester, whose 1002, one of Metrolink's original twin-cars, is seen in the city centre en route to Whitefield in 1993. (K. A. Jenkinson)

Still wishing to use their own municipal power stations, a number of tram operators took the decision to replace them with trolleybuses which, although using overhead wires for their electricity power collection, were more flexible than the trams as a result of not being subjected to running on fixed tracks, thus reducing the expenditure of their renewal. Experiments were carried out at Hendon in September 1909 using the Cedes-Stoll system which comprised the bus being connected with a flexible wire to a four-wheel trolley which ran on top of the two wires. Although this caused a number of problems if the flexible wire accidentally disconnected from the bus, surprisingly in 1913 Keighley Corporation adopted this system and was the only operator to do so, but soon abandoned it in favour of the more traditional type which used two roof-mounted trolley booms that ran underneath the twin wires. The latter first made their passenger-carrying debut in the UK in the cities of Leeds and Bradford on 20 June 1911. While Leeds abandoned this form of transport in July 1928 having never grown its system, Bradford majorly developed its route network and survived until 26 March 1972, becoming the UK's last trolleybus operator as well as its first. Prior to Bradford's closure, however, conventional trolleybuses had also operated in a number of other towns and cities across the UK, and like trams are still popular and widely used in several countries across Europe and further afield.

In the meantime, development in petrol-fuelled internal combustion engine private cars had begun, and in the late 1890s the first buses to be thus propelled began to appear. Starting in Edinburgh where they made their debut in May 1898, and then in London in October 1899, three years later the first examples fitted with rubber tyres (solid) were introduced. Regarded as being successful, UK and overseas manufacturers began to produce chassis suitable for fitting with single- and double-deck bodies and very quickly these became familiar across the whole of the UK.

Prior to the above, in 1906 Maidstone-based W. A. Stevens, who had built its first petrol-electric (hybrid) vehicle, entered into a contract with Hallford to convert its petrol engine chassis to this new form of propulsion in which the engine powered an electric generator that passed current to a traction motor that drove the rear wheels. Then, after being purchased by Thomas Tilling, in 1911 the Tilling Stevens petrol-electric TTA1 omnibus was launched, and proving more popular than 100 per cent battery-electric vehicles, sounded the death knell of the latter. The chassis of the petrol-electrics were initially built at Peckham and the bodies at Camberwell before production was moved to, and standardized, at the Tilling Stevens factory at Maidstone. Here it continued until 1930 when Thomas Tilling separated itself from Tilling Stevens, who renamed itself TS Motors Ltd. With little or no thought about pollution in those days, for the next half a century the internal combustion petrol engine remained supreme until the diesel engine made its debut and began to reduce operating costs.

Not being confined to rails or wires, this new form of mechanical transport proved to be far more flexible than trams, and not needing any infrastructure reduced operators' costs dramatically. In 1909 London General Omnibus Co. built sixty open-top double-deck buses with bodies based on horse bus designs and followed these with the ubiquitous B-type which seated eighteen passengers on the upper deck and fourteen downstairs. During the First World War, around 900 of these buses were commandeered by the War Department, who dispatched a large number of them for use by the British army in France and Belgium whilst others were fitted with lorry bodies like numerous buses requisitioned from independent bus operators around the UK. Additionally, in a bid to save petrol during the war years, several operators fitted their buses with roof-mounted bags to carry uncompressed coal-gas to provide propulsion.

Seen here being demonstrated to Hove Corporation in 1909 is this Cedes-Stoll trackless trolleybus. (Author's collection)

Keighley Corporation was the only UK operator to purchase Cedes-Stoll trolleybuses, one of which is seen here in 1914. (Keighley News)

Along with Bradford, Leeds Corporation was the first UK operator of trolleybuses in 1911. Pictured here is Railless Electric Traction 503 which had a Hurst Nelson body mounted on an Onion chassis. (Author's collection)

Replacing Keighley Corporation Cedes-Stoll trolleybuses in 1924 were a number of double- and single-deck Straker-Clough vehicles, one of which, No.10 (WT7106), is seen here when brand new. (Keighley News)

Seen here preserved at Sandtoft Trolleybus Museum is ex-London Transport 1348 (EXV348), an all-Leyland three-axle vehicle that was new in 1939. (K. A. Jenkinson)

Pictured here is Britain's last trolleybus, Bradford City Transport 844 (FWX914), suitably decorated for its final journey on 26 March 1972. It began life in 1948 as a single-decker with Mexborough & District and was given its new East Lancs double-deck body in 1962. (F. W. York collection)

Fitted with a replica body in 1996, solid-tyred Tilling Stevens petrol-electric TS3A XL1204 had started life in London with Thomas Tilling in July 1922. (F. W. York collection)

Supplied new to Harrogate & District Road Car Co. in 1924 was this Tilling-bodied solid-tyred Tilling Stevens petrol-electric TS3. (West Yorkshire Road Car Co.)

Seen here is London General B-type B5015 (LU8011) which was new in 1917. (T. M. Leach collection)

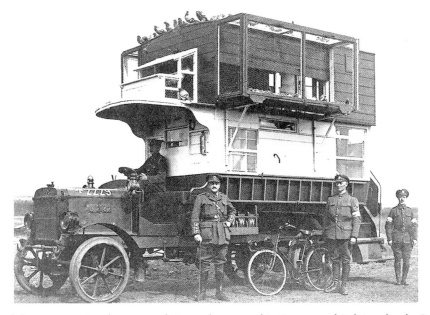

One of the many ex-London General B-type buses used in France and Belgium by the British Army in the First World War. This example is serving as a pigeon loft. (F. W. York collection)

Pictured in the First World War fitted with gas bags on their roofs are Midland Red Tilling Stevens TS3 petrol-electric single-deckers OA7091 and OA7096. (F. W. York collection)

When the war thankfully ended, a large number of these commandeered buses and lorries were sold in Britain by the War Department, resulting in numerous new bus companies being set up by former military personnel who had gained mechanical and driving skills during the conflict. Sounding the death knell to horse buses, these and newer models launched by chassis manufacturers increased year on year and as their mechanical development continued, they became more and more reliable. The versatility of these chassis enabled numerous small operators, particularly those in rural areas, to use them in a dual-purpose role for the carriage of passengers on day excursions or private hire duties and haulage duties at other times. Then, in the mid- to late 1920s, models with a lower chassis frame were introduced to make passenger boarding and alighting easier, while pneumatic tyres had replaced those of solid rubber to give a more comfortable ride.

Although the new petrol-engined buses were seen as 'the future' with little or no environmental concerns at the end of the nineteenth century, vehicle manufacturers had nevertheless started to look at other forms of propulsion and in 1897 had turned its attention to battery-powered vehicles, amongst the first of which were taxi cabs launched in London. As far as is known, the first battery-electric buses to be operated in Britain made their debut when twenty open-top thirty-four-seat double-deckers built by Electric Van, Wagon, & Omnibus Co., West Norwood, London, were placed in service on 15 July 1907 by Electrobus Co., London, on a route from Victoria station to Liverpool Street. Fitted with a Thomson Houston electric motor and powered by Tudor Accumulator Co. lead acid batteries, which were carried in a cradle beneath the floor, they could be changed in less than ten minutes and had a range of 40 miles between charges. Sadly, however, due to financial difficulties Electrobus went into liquidation on 3 January 1910. Meanwhile, Brighton, Hove & Preston Omnibus Co. had also begun operating battery-electric buses in June 1909 with four new Electric Van, Wagon, & Omnibus Co. double-deckers, and added eight more which in 1910 were acquired from Electrobus, London. Although the last of these were withdrawn from service in April 1917, York Corporation Tramways had, however, taken a late decision to enter the battery-electric market when on 20 March 1915 it placed in service four single-deckers built by Edison & Swan Electric Light Company. Weighing 4 tons and having a top speed of 12 mph, these were considered to be successful and remained in service until 1920 when they were replaced by conventional trolleybuses. Similarly, Lancaster and South Shields Corporations also purchased Brush-bodied Edison & Swan battery (accumulator) buses of the same type.

Showing the tiered seating of some early charabancs, this AA (All American) example, registered C56, started life in 1913. (Author's collection)

Typifying a solid-tyred charabanc with its canvas roof folded down is this 1913 example bodied by small Otley (West Yorkshire) coachbuilder Nicholson. (Author's collection)

New in 1907, LN708 was a battery-powered double-decker built at West Norwood by Electric Van, Wagon, & Omnibus Co., and was operated by London independent Electrobus Co. (F. W. York collection)

One of York Corporation's four Brush-bodied Edison & Swan battery (accumulator) buses, which were new in 1915, is seen here replenishing its batteries at the city's Clifton Green electric vehicle charging station. (Author's collection)

Meanwhile, after being taken over by the Underground Group in 1912, London General had separated its bus construction at Walthamstow into a separate company named AEC which was later developed to build buses for other operators across the UK. In 1923 London General opened new workshops at Chiswick to which its bodybuilding activities were transferred, this continuing until 1942. Prior to this, in 1908, Bristol Tramways began building its own buses, as too in 1923 did Birmingham & Midland Motor Omnibus Co. (BMMO) who started constructing chassis and bodies to its own design at its Bearwood workshops. Although the majority of these were built for its own use, before the Second World War it also sold some to other BET subsidiaries but ceased bodybuilding in 1969 and chassis construction a year later. In 1931 Bristol Tramways was taken over by Thomas Tilling who also bought Eastern Counties Omnibus Company, who in addition to being an operator continued to build bodies at Lowestoft (where they had been built by United Automobile Services since 1920), becoming Eastern Coach Works Ltd in 1936. This led to numerous Bristol chassis being fitted with ECW bodies and continued after Tilling was nationalized in 1948. However, a couple of years later, Bristol and ECW removed their products from the open market and then only supplied them to the nationalized former Tilling companies. After being acquired by British Leyland, Bristol and ECW were able to sell their products on the open market again, but ultimately Bristol ceased production in 1983 while ECW followed suit in 1987. Prior to this, in 1972 the National Bus Company and British Leyland had formed a joint bus manufacturing company at a new factory at Lilyhall, Whitehaven, and began building the module-constructed Leyland National which was forced on almost all NBC operators but was also available on the open market, and launched the integrally built double-deck Leyland Titan in 1975, with the Lynx replacing the National in 1985.

Illustrating the fact that early goods vehicle chassis could equally be used for passenger vehicles as they had been from before the Second World War, in 1924 the Worthing Motor Omnibus Co. developed a single-deck bus named Tramocar based on a Shelvoke & Drewry Freighter low-loading chassis that was customarily used for waste disposal trucks. Initially fitted with small solid-tyre wheels and tiller steering, the first of these small buses operated on a service along Worthing seafront where they were ultimately joined by others with pneumatic tyres and conventional wheel steering. Only thirteen of these buses were built, however, with the last remaining in service in 1942, four years after the company had been purchased by Southdown Motor Services.

Over the years, regulations on vehicle dimensions were periodically changed to allow buses and coaches to become longer and wider, with several of the former having twin rear axles to meet weight regulations. Among the first of these were London General's LS double-deckers introduced in 1927, these leading to AEC's Renowns appearing in 1929 and to tri-rear axle Leyland Tigers. In addition, in 1937 Leyland built a new front-engined twin-steering axle chassis named the Gnu and followed this in 1940 with a solitary example with underfloor engine – the Panda. In 1938 Leyland built a solitary chassisless twin front axle double-deck trolleybus which, after being used as a demonstrator, was sold to London Transport. It was not until early 1963, however, that any further twin steer passenger vehicles appeared when Bedford launched its VAL model which could be fitted with either coach or bus bodywork, this remaining in production until 1972, by which time 2,175 had been built. After a gap of more than three decades, as a result of new weight and length dimensions being introduced to enable the use of buses and coaches of 13.8-metre length, new tri-axle models were launched in the UK, with the latter of the two rear axles being steerable to improve manoeuvrability, and these quickly became popular with operators.

Built by its operator Bristol Tramways in the latter years of the 1920s, the B-type had pneumatic tyres, a lower-framed chassis, and its engine alongside the driver, as illustrated here by 'coach' bodied 378. (F. W. York collection)

Built by its owner Northern General, the SE6 was a three-axle, side-engined bus, which in the case of CN6626 was bodied by Short Bros and made its debut in service in 1935. (R. H. G. Simpson)

New to West Yorkshire Road Car Co., DB59 (JWY223) was an ECW lowbridge-bodied Bristol KS6B new in November 1950. (Alex Lawson)

Typifying the Leyland National is Ribble 451 (NTC631M) which was new in December 1973 and is seen here in Preston bus station. (K. A. Jenkinson)

Preserved at Amberley Chalk Pits Museum is this replica of a 1924 eighteen-seat Shelvoak & Drewry Tramocar originally operated in Worthing. (F. W. York collection)

Built on a tri-axle ADC chassis in 1927 and given a body built by its operator, London General LS2 (YU1166) was later converted to open staircase configuration. (F. W. York collection)

Leyland Gnu HVW214, with the model's three-axle front steering and thirty-nine-seat Duple body, started life with City Coach Co., Brentwood, in August 1939, and later passed to Eastern National via Westcliff-on-Sea Motor Services. (Author's collection)

In 1963 Bedford introduced the VAL with its twin steering front axles, and seen here is Plaxton-bodied DJH742G which was new to Thompson, London N18, in February 1969. (F. W. York)

Go-Ahead Northern's Caetano-bodied tri-axle Scania K340EB6 7097 (FJ08KLX), which was new in July 2008, clearly shows its steerable trailing rear axle in use. (T. M. Leach collection/ Mike Hutton)

Although experiments on diesel engines had begun in the first decade of the twentieth century, it was not until 1929 that the first of these power units was fitted to a passenger vehicle chassis when Gardner installed a four-cylinder unit into a Lancia chassis. After successfully being trialled in service and further developed, the diesel engine began to be installed in vehicles produced by such major chassis manufacturers as AEC, Leyland, Crossley and Bristol, and by the mid-1930s was becoming as popular as its petrol counterparts, partly due to its lower fuel consumption and related operating costs. At this time, all engines were front mounted, but in 1932 AEC produced a model, the Q type, which had its engine side mounted on the offside of the chassis behind the front axle, as too did the Northern General tri-axle SE6 appearing in 1934. Then, in 1937 the underfloor engine was introduced when Leyland built a single-deck chassis for London Transport (TF-class), and in 1938 followed it with a vertical rear-engine model – again for London Transport – (CR-class), this ultimately being slowly developed in the 1950s for double-deckers too. During the mid- to late 1930s Leyland built some chassisless trolleybuses for London Transport on which the running units were fixed to the underside of their bodies, and later in 1945 Beadle of Dartford began producing monocoque (integral chassisless) buses (often using parts taken from withdrawn pre-war buses), while as the years progressed, several leading manufacturers began producing models using this type of construction including London's Routemasters. Immediately after the ending of the Second World War, Midland Red had begun building more conventional underfloor chassis on which the engine was horizontally mounted centrally between the axles, this being copied by AEC, Leyland and other manufacturers from 1949. In 1962 underfloor horizontally mounted rear engine chassis were introduced when Bristol launched its first, the RE, which was soon followed by models from other manufacturers.

New in 1930, Barton Transport was believed to be the first operator to fit a diesel engine to a passenger-carrying vehicle, the bus concerned being the Lancia shown here. (Author's collection)

With the grille covering its side engine clearly seen, London Transport Park Royal-bodied AEC Q CLE191 (Q168) was new in August 1936 and is pictured here in its early post-Second World War livery. (F. W. York collection)

New to London Transport in July 1939, own-bodied TF77 (FJJ774) was an underfloor-engined Leyland Tiger FEC. (Author's collection)

Unique to London Transport, who purchased forty-nine of these little buses between 1937 and 1940, CR16 (FXT122) was a rear-engined Leyland Cub new in November 1939. (Ian Smith)

Integrally constructed as a prototype by Beadle using Dennis mechanical components and a Gardner 4LK engine, FNG818 was supplied new to Eastern Counties in May 1947. (T. M. Leach collection)

The prototype Routemaster, RM1 (SLT56), which was chassisless and new in September 1954, is seen here after being preserved and given a later-style radiator grille. (K. A. Jenkinson)

Starting life in November 1948, Duple-bodied underfloor-engined BMMO C1 KHA301 is pictured here in June 2022 superbly restored and preserved. (K. A. Jenkinson)

Typifying the underfloor rear-engined ECW-bodied Bristol RE is West Yorkshire 1399 (NWU324M), which was new in December 1973. (W. Counter)

As far as transmission is concerned, after early buses were fitted with a manual crash gearbox, this was slowly refined with the introduction of constant mesh and then synchromesh, all of which were to make life easier for drivers, and then in the early 1930s the pre-selector gearbox made its debut. Later in the decade Leyland introduced the gearless bus, which used a torque converter invented by Lysholm-Smith in 1928, although this was never particularly popular with operators and was abandoned at the outbreak of the Second World War. Although manual gearboxes remained the norm until the mid-1950s, and are still fitted to a few coach models today, a move was made towards electrically operated semi-automatic gearboxes and then fully automatics with some, such as those fitted in London's Routemasters, being of dual mode, allowing drivers to change at will from semi- to full-automatic control in urban and rural surrounds. Meanwhile, hybrid and battery-electric vehicles have no need for a gearbox as such and are instead controlled through their electric motors.

Until the end of 1939, the average life for buses largely employed on urban services was eight to ten years, but the advent of the Second World War changed this when PSV manufacturers were forced to turn their attention to producing military vehicles, aircraft, and armament and cease their normal work. Although chassis already under production were allowed to be finished, it was not until 1942 that bus chassis were again allowed to be built, but only by Guy and Bedford who were joined by Daimler a year later. Due to the unavailability of new vehicles except for those allocated by the Ministry of Supply to operators dependent on their needs, the existing eight–ten-year-old buses had to continue in use throughout the Second World War and for a few years beyond before they were able to be withdrawn from service.

Meanwhile, similar to the First World War, liquid fuel shortages resulted in gas-powered buses again entering the scene in 1942, although on this occasion, rather than using town gas, the gas production unit consisted of a burner unit mounted on a trailer attached to the rear of the chassis. Finding that buses equipped with these coke or anthracite burning contraptions were slow and underpowered on hills, they were never welcomed by operators, and were withdrawn by early 1945, the buses concerned then being returned to normal petrol-engined propulsion.

Illustrating that this all-Leyland Tiger TS7 is fitted with a Lysholm Smith torque converter is this Rawtenstall Corporation all-Leyland TS7 displaying 'Gearless Bus' lettering on its radiator grille. (Author's collection)

Typical of Guy's wartime buses is this London Transport Arab II with its snout radiator and Park Royal body, seen here preserved and superbly restored. (F. W. York collection)

The only new single-deck buses built during the Second World War were Bedford OWBs, one of which is ex-Northern Ireland Road Transport Board GZ783 which dates from September 1942 and carries a correct replica body. (K. A. Jenkinson)

Typifying the time-expired buses which continued to run throughout the Second World War is this Bradford Corporation lowbridge Leyland TD1, the bonnet of which had been extended to allow a retro-fitted Gardner diesel engine to be accommodated. (R. F. Mack)

This diagram shows in detail how a gas-producing trailer worked when coupled to double- and single-deck buses during the Second World War. (Author's collection)

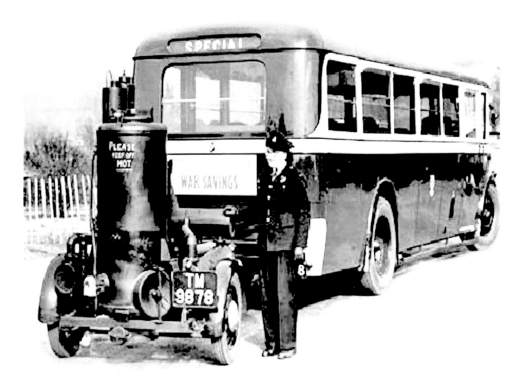

Various styles of gas-producing trailer units were used during the Second World War, depending on the manufacturer. This example is seen in 1942 attached to Luton Corporation Duple-bodied Daimler CH6 TM9878 which was new in February 1932. (Author's collection)

Southdown 1933 vintage Short-bodied Leyland TD2 952 (UF8852), seen here in Portsmouth in the Second World War hauling another style of gas-producing trailer, is overtaking a loaned London Transport Tilling ST while one of the city's trolleybuses is seen in the distance. (F. W. York collection)

Looking at the bodywork fitted to buses and coaches, these were originally constructed on wooden frames, but in 1931 Metro Cammell offered steel framework as an alternative, this being copied by other coachbuilders a few years afterwards. As the years rolled by, metal frames became the norm and gradually replaced wood as the element of choice and with lighter materials such as aluminium, glass-fibre and plastic ultimately being introduced, all of this greatly reduced vehicle weight. Due to lower-frame chassis making their appearance in the 1920s, it became possible to reduce the height of double-deck bodies by over 12 inches when in 1927 Leyland introduced a design in which a side gangway was fitted which protruded into the lower deck while the seats on the upper deck were arranged on benches for four passengers. This enabled operators to use double-deckers on services which passed under bridges lower than 14 feet 6 inches – the normal height for twin-deck buses. Later, in 1949 in an effort to build low-height double-deckers without needing a sunken upper-deck gangway, Bristol designed a lower chassis which could accommodate a body with a conventional central upper-deck gangway, and named this the Lodekka. After two buses of this design were trialled in service, the Lodekka went into full production in 1953 and later, in 1958, it was also built under licence by Dennis who identified it as the Loline. The success of this design inspired AEC to produce an integrally built low-floor double-deck in 1965 named the Bridgemaster, which in 1963 was also offered with a separate chassis as the Renown. While the Dennis and AEC models remained in production until 1967, Bristol's Lodekka survived for a further year before being discontinued.

As coach designs became more stylish and luxurious, a small number of bodybuilders introduced a new design known as the observation coach featuring a raised rear section to give passengers a better forward view. This design was also used in 1936 by London Transport for eight forward control Leyland Cubs employed on interrail station duties, the space below the raised section being used for passengers' luggage. This body style was also used from 1946 on normal control Commer Commando chassis by the RAF for crew transport and some airlines for airport shuttle duties, but never gained great popularity on conventional chassis for coach operators. In 1952 a further deck and a half design for airport work appeared on which the raised portion was extended forward along the full length of the body.

The upper deck of a 1932 ECOC-bodied lowbridge bus clearly shows the four-in-a-row seats and offside sunken gangway. (K. A. Jenkinson)

The lower deck of the same bus illustrates the projecting sunken upper-deck gangway which caused passengers to lower their head when leaving their seats. (K. A. Jenkinson)

The second prototype Bristol Lodekka, new in March 1950, is seen here with its sole owner, West Yorkshire Road Car Co., after spending time as a Bristol demonstrator. (W. Counter)

The lower-deck interior of the ECW-bodied Bristol Lodekka, seen above, shows its rear-facing full-width front seat. (ECW)

Seen here in preservation is East Yorkshire Park Royal-bodied low-height AEC Renown CKH782C, which was new in April 1965 and was its chassis manufacturer's answer to the Bristol Lodekka. (John Law)

London Transport's forward control Leyland Cub CLE548, new in October 1936, carried a twenty-seat Park Royal body which had a raised rear section under which plenty of space was given for luggage. (Nigel Eadon-Clarke)

Seen here fitted with a luxurious full-fronted Whitson observation coach body is an AEC Regal III dating from 1950. (Author's collection)

Constructed to a deck and a half layout, MLL738 was one of sixty-five AEC Regal IVs built by Park Royal for British European Airways in 1952/3 for passenger transfers between Central London and Heathrow Airport. (Nigel Eadon-Clarke)

Although a few overseas manufacturers' products including the USA's Model T Ford, Reo and Chevrolet, etc., had been imported into the UK during the 1920s and '30s, mainly for use as small coaches or country buses, almost all the passenger-carrying vehicles built over the next three decades were produced by UK manufacturers, and it was not until the 1960s that what was to become a foreign invasion began to enter the scene. Amongst the first of these overseas companies were coachbuilders Caetano and Jonckheere, and chassis builders Scania, Mercedes-Benz, DAF, and Volvo, who gingerly dipped their toes into the water. Since the 1970s, the floodgates steadily opened and have grown considerably following the demise of almost all of the UK producers.

In the meantime, several of the well-known UK manufacturers had been the subject of takeovers and began to disappear, with Albion being taken over by Leyland in 1951 and although continuing until 1982, its name was dropped in 1972. Similarly, AEC, who had produced bus chassis since 1912 and joined forces with Leyland to produce BUT trolleybuses in 1946, acquired Crossley and Maudslay in 1948 and was ultimately acquired by Leyland in 1962 and vanished in 1979 when production stopped at its Southall factory. Daimler did not enter the British Leyland fold until 1981 after passing through Jaguar Cars in 1960 and British Motor Corporation in 1966. Prior to this, in 1948 AEC had been a founder of Associated Vehicle Sales which in the following year took over the coachbuilding activities of Chas. H. Roe and Park Royal. Similarly, Bristol Commercial Vehicles and Eastern Coach Works were both completely swallowed up by Leyland, who had gained a 50 per cent share in 1969, with the former closing in 1983 and the latter in 1987. These were not the only UK chassis manufacturers to disappear from the scene, however, as Guy, who had built bus chassis since 1914 and had bought Sunbeam Commercial Vehicles in 1948, passed to Jaguar Cars in 1966 and then British Leyland in 1968 and saw its name dropped in 1972 and its factory close in 1982. Also disappearing was

Foden, who ceased bus chassis production in 1956 but then briefly reappeared in 1976 when it introduced a semi-integral double-deck chassis. Sadly only eight were built, one of which was retained for further development while six of the others were bodied by Northern Counties and one by East Lancs. The model was abandoned in 1978 and the company sold to USA-based Paccar two years later. A more recent incomer to bus manufacturing was Seddon, who began building passenger chassis in 1946 and continued until 1982 and also constructed bodies through its Pennine Coachcraft subsidiary from around 1960. For lightweight vehicles built in the UK, Commer, Ford, and Bedford were the most prolific, with the latter two disappearing from the scene in 1986, and the former in the 1970s.

Sadly, in more recent times almost all of the major UK bus manufacturers were ultimately sold to overseas owners with Leyland being acquired by Volvo in 1988. Passing to India-based Ashok Leyland in 2019 was Optare (renamed Switch Mobility in 2020) who had been born from the ashes of Chas H. Roe in 1985 and over the years had been part of United Bus (DAF) from 1990 to 1993 before being acquired by Hungarian manufacturer NABI from 2000 to 2005, and then the Darwin Group from 2008 to 2019. Following the above, Alexander Dennis, which was formed from Transbus in 2004 who owned Dennis, Alexander, and Plaxton, was sold to Canadian bus builder New Flyer Industries. Today, after all the crown jewels had been sold to overseas owners, the only recognized bus manufacturers remaining in the UK are Wrightbus in Northern Ireland, which was established in 1946 and purchased by Ryse Energy owner Jo Bamford in 2019, and Mellor Coachcraft, Rochdale, who had entered the market in the 1960s.

Typifying the 1920s Ford T-type is this bus-bodied example operated in the Bristol area. (Author's collection)

Amongst the early overseas coachbuilders to appear in the UK was Caetano, Portugal, whose bodywork is seen here on this Ford R1114 owned by Birmingham independent Claribels. (Author's collection)

Another European manufacturer to enter the UK market was Spanish coachbuilder Irizar, whose unusual styling with raised rear part is seen here on a Volvo B58 chassis, new in 1981 to Steve Stockdale, Selby. (Franz Angevaare)

In 1969 Swedish manufacturer Scania joined forces with Metro Cammel Weymann to produce an integral single-decker, seen here, named the Metro-Scania. (K. S. E. Till)

Both the coaches seen here in December 2008, owned by City Travel, Cullingworth, Bradford, feature foreign chassis and coachwork. On the left, V323EAL, which was new in November 1999, is a MAN 18.310 carrying Noge bodywork while alongside it is YO02LHZ (originally registered RE02ANN), a Beaulas-bodied Iveco 391E EuroRider 35. (K. A. Jenkinson)

New in December 1932 to W. Alexander & Son, now preserved Albion Valkyrie PW65 WG1448 has an Alexander body that was built in 1945. (K. A. Jenkinson)

With its body built by its chassis manufacturer, Crossley, and featuring its traditional-style rear side windows on both decks, this example was one of six purchased by Bradford City Transport in September 1948. (R. F. Mack)

Although Maudslay had been purchased by AEC in 1948, a year later it still badged its products under its old name, as illustrated by this Park Royal-bodied Marathon III of Scottish operator MacBrayne, to whom it was new in August 1949. (The Reid family)

With both its chassis and body builders passing to Associated Vehicle Sales control in 1948, Leeds City Transport Roe-bodied AEC Regent III 425 (LUA425) is seen here in Guiseley a year earlier. (R. F. Mack)

With its chassis and body built by the same manufacturer, Seddon, Pennine RU OFM800K was one of 100 buses of this type purchased by Crosville in 1971. (Martyn Hearson)

New in July 1949, Murgatroyd of Thruscross's HWY778 is a Plaxton-bodied Commer Avenger. (K. A. Jenkinson)

Typifying the ever-popular Duple Vega-bodied Bedford SB, now preserved LGV994 was new in March 1958. (Nigel Eadon-Clarke)

One of only seven Foden NC double-deckers built, Northern Counties-bodied TUG250R was supplied new to West Yorkshire PTE in March 1977 and is seen here after entering preservation. (Martyn Hearson)

In the early 1970s the need for small passenger-carrying vehicles useful for operating on stage carriage services through congested housing estates, etc., led to the introduction of minibuses largely based on Ford Transit and Freight Rover Sherpa local delivery vans, which were colloquially known as bread vans. Initially the bodies of these were converted into sixteen-seat buses by a number of small coachbuilders such as Dormobile, Carlyle and PMT (who was also an operator), but in the mid-1980s, as well as specialists Reeve Burgess and Robin Hood, some larger manufacturers such as Alexander, East Lancs, and Northern Counties entered the fray and ultimately introduced custom-built bodies with larger carrying capacities on Mercedes-Benz, Iveco, and Dodge/Renault van chassis and cowls. Prior to these, in 1978 Bedford, in conjunction with Marshalls, Cambridge, surprisingly designed and built a larger twenty-four-seat transverse rear-engined minibus (or perhaps more correctly a midibus).

Returning to environmental issues and with fuel costs rising and the need to reduce pollution more urgent than ever, the government slowly started to look at forms of battery-electric propulsion as a means of reducing carbon emissions, and to this end the Department of Trade and Industry offered support to manufacturers developing such vehicles. Amongst the first was Crompton Leyland Electricars, Tredegar (owned by Hawker Siddeley Group and BLMC), who in 1972 built two battery-electric midibuses for demonstration to operators across the UK. Based on a Leyland 900 FG commercial chassis with bodywork by Willowbrook, they had lead acid batteries and an unladen weight of 7.75 tons. Of 22-foot length, 8-foot 1-inch width, and 9-foot 6-inch height, the prototype only seated nine and had standing capacity for seventeen. With a range of 35 miles between charges in city centre traffic, they could supposedly travel 70 miles non-stop, and their battery sets were rapidly interchangeable. Although Crompton did not pursue its production of PSVs, it did continue to manufacture battery-powered milk floats and similar vehicles. Soon afterwards, Seddon rose to the challenge and in conjunction with battery manufacturer Chloride, in December 1973 built a Pennine RU with this form of propulsion, following it in February 1975 with a nineteen-seat Pennine IV midibus similarly equipped by Lucas, both of which were trialled with SELNEC PTE. In the meantime, the Department for Environment also commissioned Leyland and the NBC to convert a Leyland National to battery propulsion with a 360-volt traction motor, but unlike the earlier experiments this carried its Chloride batteries (which are understood to have weighed 6.9 tons!) in a two-axle trailer towed behind the bus. The bus chosen was a 1973 Ribble example, but when it emerged in February 1975, due to its length it was not permitted to operate on the public highway and instead was intermittently employed by Crosville on the Runcorn Busway from September of that year to February 1978. However, despite all of these experiments being reasonably successful, no further trials took place, and it was not until two decades later that any more battery-electric passenger-carrying vehicles were placed in service in the UK.

The next development as far as the UK was concerned, although not environment related, was the introduction of the articulated vehicle (bendibus) which had been common across Europe and other places around the world for many years. After unsuccessful experiments with articulated trailer buses being undertaken in the Second World War, the first appearance of conventional bendibuses in Britain did not come until August 1978 when South Yorkshire PTE took an MAN for demonstration, following it with four more together with five Leyland-DABs in 1979/80. Also purchasing Leyland-DABs in 1981 was British Airways, who received seven Roe-bodied examples in 1981 and then SYPTE took another thirteen in 1985. Then in 1981 Mercedes-Benz entered the UK bendibus market, as did Volvo in 1998 and Scania in 2003, and only popular with a few operators, the articulated bubble burst in the second decade of the twenty-first century leaving only a conventional handful still in service in 2024 except for the eighteen new Gliders introduced in Belfast in 2018.

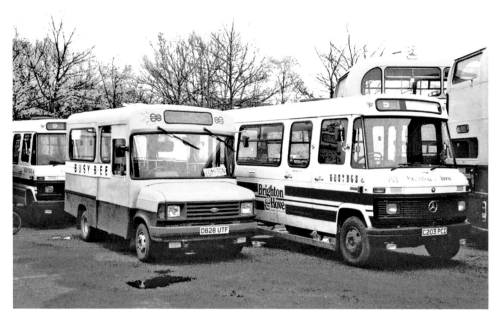

Illustrating two early deregulation minibuses, Carlyle-converted Ford Transit 'bread van' D828UTF new to Alder Valley in October 1986 stands alongside 'custom-built' Alexander-bodied Mercedes-Benz L608D C201PCD which started life with Brighton & Hove in December 1985. (K. A. Jenkinson)

New to Newport Transport in January 1987, D805MNY is a custom-built East Lancs-bodied Dodge S56. (K. A. Jenkinson)

With its tri-axle chassis and body both built by Talbot, Pullman E571MAC, seen here in preservation, was new to Barrow Borough Transport in June 1988. (T. M. Leach collection)

Representing the Omni minibuses built by CVE and its successors is F722YOV, which was new in October 1988. (John Law)

Starting life as a demonstrator in November 1978, AVS903T is one of only four Marshall-bodied Bedford JJLs built. (K. A. Jenkinson)

A model that became popular over three decades was the integrally built Metrorider, introduced by MCW in 1986 and later taken over by Optare. (K. A. Jenkinson)

Pictured while being trialled by South Yorkshire PTE is Crompton Leyland Electricars battery-electric-powered demonstrator 1000 (CWO516K). (Author's collection)

Battery-powered Seddon Pennine RU XVU387M with Pennine bodywork was new in December 1973 and is seen here carrying promotional lettering with Greater Manchester PTE, who numbered it EX61. (Barry Newsome collection)

With its twin-axle battery trailer attached, Ribble Leyland National OTF354M is seen here at Runcorn while on loan to Crosville in 1975. (Barry Newsome collection)

The battery pack in the trailer hauled by Ribble Leyland National OTF354M can be clearly seen here. (Barry Newsome collection)

New in August 1978 as a demonstrator for its manufacturer, sixty-three-seat MAN SG192 bendibus was later operated in Sheffield by South Yorkshire PTE. (Author's collection)

New to First York in May 2006 but seen here after its transfer to Bradford is Wright-bodied Volvo B7LA streetcar 19010 (YK06AUA), a model that was exclusive to FirstBus and built to its specification. (K. A. Jenkinson)

New to Translink Citybus, Belfast, in July 2018, Van Hool forty-six-seat articulated Glider 3220 (HGZ8220) is seen here in service when only a few months old. (Author's collection)

In a bid to speed up tram services, in the 1920s several cities across the UK laid the track on some routes on grassed or paved areas in the centre or side of wide, normal roads, thus separating them from other forms of road transport. Known as 'reserved track', as opposed to 'street running', many survived until the final withdrawal of the trams. Then, in 1984, with attention being given to non-railed transport, as an experiment Birmingham launched a trial busway which similarly separated buses from the rest of the road using a system where they were guided by concrete kerbs, with the buses themselves being fitted with a guide wheel forward of the front wheel. In Birmingham's case, the vehicles thus equipped were fourteen new MCW Metrobuses painted in a silver livery and branded Tracline for the 65 route. Although reasonably successful and serving the purpose for which it was intended, the trial ended in 1987, after which the guidance kerbs were removed and the road was returned to a normal thoroughfare. However, in 1995 after having seen the Birmingham trial and a similar system in Essen, Germany, Leeds built a guided busway along Scott Hall Road, and, proving successful, this led to a similar one being constructed in 2001 on a long stretch of York Road. This was copied in the same year along Manchester Road, Bradford, and all three are still operational today. A number of other guided busways were introduced in Crawley, Cambridgeshire, Kesgrave (Ipswich), Leigh, and Edinburgh, all of which are still in use. In addition to kerb-guided busways, which are unable to be used by other vehicles, despite bus lanes having been painted on the surface of numerous roads around the UK, and are camera protected during their hours of use, these do not physically separate buses from the highway and are frequently abused by other traffic.

Although modern trams had been introduced to the UK in 1992, attention continued towards non-railed electric transport, and making its debut in the UK in 1998 was Italian manufacturer Tecnobus who was established in 1991. Its first model to appear in Britain was the Gulliver, a left-hand-drive battery-powered microbus with doors on each side and seating for nine passengers. Introduced by First Bristol and on Merseyside on short-distance city centre services, in 2002 the Gulliver was joined by the three-axle Pantheon, which also had doors on each side of its body, was again of left-hand-drive configuration and accommodated eleven seated passengers.

A Leeds City Transport 'Horsfield' tram heads along York Road in the mid-1950s on the reserved track which has now become part of the guided busway. (T. M. Leach collection)

Seen here in Short Heath, Birmingham, in June 1984 on the UK's first guided busway for which it carries branding is West Midlands PTE MCW Metrobus 8106 (A106WVP). (WMPTE)

Heading along the dual-track York Road guided busway, Leeds, is Arriva Yorkshire Alexander-bodied Volvo B7TL 656 (W656CWX), which was new in April 2000 and is branded for the Leeds–Castleford services. (K. A. Jenkinson)

Standing inside First PMT's Rock Ferry depot is nine-seat left-hand drive Italian-built battery-electric Tecnobus S255AFA. (K. A. Jenkinson)

Selwyn, Runcorn's eleven-seat battery-powered tri-axle Tecnobus Pantheon 194 (DE52NYX), was new in November 2002. (Barry Newsome collection)

With environmental concerns gaining momentum and the introduction of low-emission and clean-air zones in several cities in the UK and across the world, vehicle manufacturers now began to examine less-polluting methods of propulsion and under EU regulations gradually refined engine emissions. It was not, however, until around the start of the twenty-first century that they began the introduction of hybrid vehicles in which the internal combustion engine and electric transmission were combined, similar in many ways to the 1920s Tilling Stevens petrol-electrics. Although Wrightbus had launched a single-deck model under the name 'Electrocity' on a Dennis Dart SLF chassis in 1998, and a second example based on a DAF SB120 in 2002, these were, in fact, diesel-electric hybrid vehicles rather than petrol-electrics and were used for developments which began to change market perception. Attention towards hybrid buses continued to grow as the first decade of the twenty-first century progressed and in 2008 Alexander Dennis launched its single-deck Enviro200H hybrid chassis which was followed by the double-deck Enviro400H which, later in 2018, offered a variant that replaced batteries with BAE Systems ultracapacitors while retaining its Cummins ISB4.5 four-cylinder diesel engine. Hot on the heels of ADL's hybrid models came Volvo's B5LH, as too did Wrightbus' integrally built Gemini 2 which used DAF DB250 components. Also of integral construction and built by Wrightbus was the NBFL double-decker which had made its debut in 2007 and was specially designed for Transport for London as its new Routemaster (colloquially known as the Borismaster), 1,000 of which were built.

Wrightbus Electrocity demonstrator AKZ7122 was a hybrid Dennis Dart SLF with Wright thirty-five-seat bodywork new in October 1998. (K. A. Jenkinson)

Travel London's Wright Electrocity hybrid 8804 (LJ57YAW) started life in November 2007. (K. A. Jenkinson)

Maytree of Bolton's fifty-seven-seat long wheelbase diesel-electric hybrid Optare Versa school bus YJ61CKC was new in December 2011. (K. S. E. Till)

The first hybrid buses purchased by First Leeds were Wright-bodied Volvo B7LHs, one of which, 39202 (BJ60BZB), new in February 2011, is seen here in its original livery. (K. A. Jenkinson)

Stagecoach Manchester Alexander Dennis E40H hybrid 12186 (MX62GFK) was new to the company in January 2013. (K. A. Jenkinson)

New to Arriva Yorkshire in March 2013, 1700 (YJ13FJY) was a low-height Wright-bodied Volvo B5LH. (K. A. Jenkinson)

New to Stagecoach Bluebird in July 2012, 29001 (SV12CZR) is a hybrid Alexander Dennis E35H, seen here in Aberdeen in 2023. (Richard Walter)

One of ten New Zealand-built Designline all-electric twenty-nine-seat Olympus midibuses built in 2005 and imported into the UK by Stagecoach Busways, 61006 (NX05PXL) is seen here in Newcastle-upon-Tyne on 9 May 2009. (K. A. Jenkinson)

Turning now to pure electric power, amongst the first to conduct experiments in this field was Cradeley Heath-based Parry People Movers who, in 2005, entered the market with its Minitram, a dual door minibus using a rapidly spinning flywheel as a store of kinetic energy which was used to power it. Although a demonstration vehicle was produced and tested in service, it was never placed in production, leaving Parry's to concentrate on its small rail units instead. Prior to this, in July 1994 Iveco built two thirteen-seat dual-door Mellor-bodied electric minibuses which were trialled in service by Bayline in Torquay before being transferred to sister company Thames Transit in Oxford. Several years later, in April 2009 Optare introduced a twenty-five-seat three-battery-electric Solo M880 twenty-five-seater using plug-in inductive charging. This paved the way for more advanced electric vehicles from the Sherburn-in-Elmet manufacturer who later launched the 9-metre and 9.7-metre Solo SR EV in 2012, these using two banks of Valence lithium ion phosphate batteries which were roof mounted and worked in tandem. Following these, in 2013 Optare introduced its all-electric Versa and then, a year later, its all-electric Metrocity single-decker. By now, a number of other bus manufacturers had also gained experience with electric propulsion and from across the Channel came the MAN Electrocity, which was first demonstrated in the UK in 2010.

Continuing the move towards full-electric buses, on 19 January 2014 Arriva the Shires began a five-year trial of eight Wrightbus all-electric StreetLites on a 17-mile service between Bletchley and Wolverton, passing through Milton Keynes en route. These buses differed from previous battery-electric vehicles by having wireless inductive charging through plates in the road at each end of the route in which wire coils generated a magnetic field which induced a voltage in the plate lowered from the bus to 4 cm above it. Equipped with a Siemens electric drive system, the buses were equipped with three lithium manganese oxide batteries, two of which were located behind the rear wheels and the other on the front area of the roof, thus giving the bus an overall height of 3.5 metres. With thirty-seven seats, the vehicles had an unladen weight of 9,720 kgs.

Then, in a bid to reduce emissions in York, in 2014 Transdev surprisingly converted a handful of its 1999 Dennis Trident open-top sightseeing buses from diesel power to all-electric, while in May of that year First York introduced six plug-in all-electric Optare Versas for operation on park & ride duties within the city, following these with a further six in 2015. Later, in 2017 Optare converted one of its MetroDecker demonstrators from diesel power to all-electric, and in 2019 supplied thirty-one EVs to Metroline, London, while during the following year First York took twenty-one for park & ride duties. These had a gvw of 18,000 kgs and featured plug-in charging with a 150-mile range between charges.

Although for a number of years it had been common across Europe and several other countries across the world including the USA, CNG didn't make its debut in the UK until June 1996 when Stagecoach put two Optare MetroRiders in service in Cambridge. Although these remained the only two buses of their type for several years, Optare retrofitted a number of Solos to CNG power for Anglian Bus and Stagecoach Lincolnshire, all of which had their biomethane tanks placed on their roofs. At around this same time, MAN launched an Ecocity single-decker demonstrator powered by renewable natural gas (biomethane, produced from landfill, food and farm waste, plus human faeces) which was carried in tanks mounted on its roof, and then, in 2013 Scania introduced its biomethane-powered K270UB which was given Enviro single-deck bodies by ADL and saw Reading and Stagecoach Busways purchasing forty each. Following these, in 2017 Scania entered the double-deck market with a bio-powered ADL-bodied N280UD, the main customers for which were Nottingham and Reading. With electric- and hydrogen-powered buses now taking the stage, it will be interesting to see whether or not the interest in biomethane-powered buses will survive the competition.

Seen at Bradford Interchange on 4 October 2005 while being demonstrated on the free city centre service operated by FirstBus is Parry People Mover's Minitram VO52AFA. (K. A. Jenkinson)

New to Bayline, Torquay, in July 1994, and later operated by Stagecoach Oxford, seen here preserved is battery-powered dual-door thirteen-seat Mellor-bodied Iveco 49.10 L247FDV. (Malcolm Crowe)

Pictured in Oxford sponsored by Southern Electric is Stagecoach-operated battery-powered eighteen-seat Optare MetroRider 804 (L804HJO) which began life with City of Oxford in November 1993. (Malcolm Crowe)

All-electric Optare SoloEV demonstrator YJ60EZR was incorrectly registered when new in April 2009 and was, in fact, YJ09EZR. (Optare)

London United dual-door all-electric Optare Versa OCE1 (LJ14SZO) was new in April 2014 and later passed to Arriva London. (F. W. York collection)

Resting on a pallet is a battery pack awaiting fitting to an Optare VersaEV. (Optare)

Seen departing from Bletchley bus station on 29 September 2014 is Arriva the Shires inductive-charged battery-electric Wrightbus Streetlite WF 5003 (KP63TDX). (K. A. Jenkinson)

Pictured on 24 July 2019 with Electricity branding on its side windows is Stagecoach Highland Country 48902 (YJ15AWF), an electric Optare SoloSR EV which made its debut in March 2015. (Richard Walter)

Believed to be the UK's first all-electric bus, Transdev York East Lancs-bodied Dennis Trident 4009 (T407SMY) started life with Metrobus as a conventional diesel bus in August 1999 and was converted to electric power in 2007. (Transdev York)

One of First York's new electric double-deckers placed in service in August 2020 is integrally built Optare MD1114EV 39510 (YJ20AXH). (K. A. Jenkinson)

Seen here on 4 December 2022 when brand new is Abellio all-electric Wrightbus StreetDeck BEV 3018 (LV72BZM). (Paul Savage)

Transport for London LT11 (LT1011 orig. LK13FJJ), seen here at the NEC, Birmingham, in November 2023 is the first Wrightbus NBFL to be retroconverted to electric power. (Richard Walter)

Seen here in Cambridge at the June 2006 launch of the city's two new gas-powered Optare MetroRiders are Stagecoach GAZ4381 and GAZ4382. (K. A. Jenkinson)

Starting life with Lincolnshire Road Car as a diesel-engined Optare Solo in April 2004, Stagecoach Lincolnshire 47273 (FX04WFT) is seen here ten years later after being retrofitted for gas propulsion. (T. M. Leach collection)

Built in November 2011 as a demonstrator, Caetano-bodied MAN NL273F Ecocity WH61HSL carried branding stating that it was propelled by pure gas. (F. W. York collection)

Biomethane-powered (human sewage and food waste) Alexander Dennis-bodied Scania K270UB demonstrator, appropriately registered YT13YUK, was new in March 2013 and is seen here in its promotional livery. (Geof Sheppard, CC BY-SA 4.0)

Also new as a demonstrator was Alexander-Dennis-bodied Scania N280UD, which made its debut in February 2017. As can be seen by its promotional branding, it was powered by biogas produced from food scraps and sewage waste. (T. M. Leach collection)

One of twenty-one ADL Enviro400 MMC-bodied CNG-powered Scania N280UDs purchased new by CT Plus, Bristol, in December 2018, all of which later passed to First West of England. (Sustainable Bus)

Despite several overseas countries having placed numerous all-electric buses in service, the UK was much slower in doing so until the government began to offer financial assistance in a bid to encourage public and commercial transport operators to purchase more emissions-free, and particularly all-electric, vehicles. With their operating range between charges steadily continuing to improve, a number of bus and coach manufacturers and operators slowly began to take an interest, particularly in areas making moves towards becoming carbon neutral. Amongst the leaders was Wrightbus, who announced its 10.6-metre-length StreetAir EV single-decker in August 2016, weighing 18 tonnes and offered with plug-in inductive (through the road surface) or conductive (with a pantograph) charging methods. After building two prototypes, the first six production buses (and only ones to date) were placed in service by Lothian Buses in October 2017, and although it was also offered as a shorter-wheelbase single-decker based on the StreetLite, and a double-decker on the StreetDeck, examples of neither of these were built and were quickly dropped from the range.

New in September 2017, SK67FLE is one of six all-electric Wrightbus StreetAir EV single-deckers with roof-mounted batteries purchased by Lothian Buses. (Richard Walter)

Seen on display at the Bus & Coach Show at the NEC, Birmingham, in November 2017 is Wrightbus's new all-electric StreetLite EV. (K. A. Jenkinson)

Also embracing electric propulsion was Chinese manufacturer BYD (Build My Dream, or Beyond My Dreams depending on which BYD publicity you have seen!) who was initially a battery manufacturer before entering the bus-building market in the first decade of the twenty-first century. Making its debut in the UK in December 2013 when it supplied two K9E dual-door single-deckers to London General for evaluation, it was, however, another two years before it gained its first orders, these being for thirteen K9E front-entrance single-deckers for Nottingham Community Transport and a K8UR dual-door single-deck demonstrator for London General. Its first double-deckers were five dual-door K8SRs delivered to Metroline in March 2016 and all these had BYD bodywork and featured plug-in charging. Joining them in 2016/7 were sixty-three D9UR single-deckers with bodywork by Alexander Dennis (with whom BYD had entered into a collaboration in 2015), these being dual-door examples for London General and single-door buses for Arriva Merseyside, 168 D8URs for several operators, and 220 D8URDD double-deckers, all the chassis for which were built overseas by BYD and employed plug-in charging. Then, in 2021 ADL began assembling BYD chassis in the UK at Falkirk, marketed the complete buses as the EnviroEV, and also offered DC charging via rising roof-mounted rails on both its single and double-deckers.

Yet another Chinese manufacturer to target the UK market was Zhengzhou Yutong Bus Company who claimed to be the largest electric bus manufacturer in the world, having produced over 100,000 before the end of 2020. After appointing Pelican Bus & Coach as its UK distributor in 2013, Yutong's first vehicles made their debut in the UK in March 2014, initially coaches fitted with its own bodywork, but in February 2017 introduced its first stage carriage vehicle, this being a 12-metre-length single-door E12 demonstrator fitted with nine battery packs on its roof, seven in its engine bay, and employed plug-in charging. After a second demonstrator entered service in London in March 2018, this time in dual-door format, orders were placed with Newport Buses for thirteen E12s, nine E10s each for Go-North East and First Leeds, and one for Scottish Power, all of which entered service between September and November 2020. In addition, a wide-bodied six-door ABe13 airside bus capable of carrying 110 passengers was delivered to Newcastle Airport, while in 2021 Scottish operators McGills and Ember respectively ordered thirty-three and six single-deckers. Prior to this, however, in October 2020 Ember placed two TCe12s in service, these being the first battery-electric coaches to operate in the UK.

A further newcomer to the UK electric bus market was Spanish manufacturer Irizar, who after supplying coach bodies mainly on Scania chassis to UK operators since 1979, and then complete coaches from 2011, introduced two dual-door i2e single-deck buses for evaluation with Go-Ahead London General in July 2015, following these with one for CT Plus, London, in November 2017, to date these being the only examples in the UK. Although all three buses used plug-in battery charging, Irizar also offered overhead pantograph charging for operators preferring this method.

Despite Volvo having launched an all-electric version of its 12-metre 7900 single-decker in Europe in 2015, it was, however, not until August 2017 that it made its debut in the UK in the form of a demonstrator. Using lithium ion batteries and employing conductive (pantograph) charging, it weighed in at 19,500 kg, but to date the only examples in operation in the UK are eight single-door buses with Transdev's Harrogate Bus Company which entered service in July 2018, and six dual-door bus examples for Birmingham Airport in December 2019. Four years later, in 2022, Volvo launched a new all-electric model designated the BZL, this being available as a double- or single-deck model with pantograph or plug-in charging. The first examples entered service at the start of 2023, all of which were fitted with MCV bodywork, although discussions are being undertaken with other coachbuilders.

London United's Alexander Dennis-bodied BYD D8UR BE37008 (LJ18FJF) is seen here on the M1 motorway in North Yorkshire on delivery to the capital in May 2018. (Rik Ward)

One of five all-BYD dual-door all-electric K8SRs supplied to Metroline, London, in 2016, BYD1475 (LJ16EZR) is seen here at an open day at Potters Bar garage on 22 July 2017. (Nigel Eadon-Clarke)

Wearing Stourton park & ride livery is First Leeds all-electric ADL Enviro400 MMC-bodied BYD D8UR-DD 388403 (LG21HZX), which was new in June 2021. (ADL)

Carrying branding for the city in which it is operating (Dunfermline) is Stagecoach Fife all-electric ADL-bodied BYD D8UR 30026 (LG23 FHT), which was new in March 2023. (Richard Walter)

Seen recharging through its roof-mounted pantograph is Go-Ahead London ADL-bodied BYD D86R-DD EP£ (LG71DZK), which was new in February 2022. (Author's collection)

Seen here undergoing plug-in charging is Arriva Merseyside ADL Enviro200EV-bodied BYD D9UR 7000 (LJ67DLX). (ADL-BYD)

On display at the NEC in 2017 is Pelican Bus & Coach's Yutong demonstrator which was new in February of that year, has a single piece roof pod, and carries a poster on its side panels stating 'plug in to the future'. (K. A. Jenkinson)

Seen when new at the NEC, Birmingham, in October 2019 before being registered YD12NGE, this all-electric Yutong E10, which has two roof pods, began life as a demonstrator before joining Stagecoach Midland Red. (K. A. Jenkinson)

Edinburgh-based Ember was the first UK operator to purchase all-electric coaches, these being Yutong TCe12s, one of which, YD70CHX, is seen here on its first day in service. (Richard Walter)

New to Nottingham Community Transport in December 2013, thirty-two-seat 941 (YD63VAE) is an all-electric Optare Versa. (Optare)

Built as a demonstrator by Irizar in September 2017, dual-door fifty-seven-seat i4h YN67VCZ was promoted as the UK's first hybrid coach. (Author's collection)

Being displayed at the Bus & Coach Show at the NEC, Birmingham, in October 2017 is this all-electric Irizar i2e demonstrator which was later registered YN67VDK. (K. A. Jenkinson)

E137 seen with its pantograph raised during the charging process is Y6BHX, one of Birmingham International Airport's six Volvo 9700E single-deckers which entered service at the end in December 2019. (Birmingham Airport)

Following the above, in 2019 Mellor Coachcraft of Rochdale proudly announced what it claimed was the first all-electric minibus built in the world. This was the front-wheel-drive low-floor Orion E which was available on a Fiat Ducato chassis, had an overall length of 7.9 metres, and was powered by two roof-mounted batteries with plug-in charging. Having seating for up to sixteen passengers, although it was largely directed at the community transport market, it was also available as a conventional vehicle without doors in its rear bulkhead. Then, in 2022 Mellor launched its Sigma range, an integrally built all-electric single-decker of which initially there were three variants: the Sigma 7, which seated fifteen passengers; the twenty-seven-seat Sigma 8; and the thirty-five-seat Sigma 10. At the time of writing, eight Sigmas had been produced, two of which were supplied to Holkham Hall Estate and two to Shuttle Buses, Kilwinning, while the remaining four were used by Mellor as demonstrators.

Then, another Chinese bus builder entered the scene in 2020 when Higer Bus Company introduced its integrally constructed battery-electric 'Steen' single-decker to the UK market. The history of Higer dates back to 1998 when it began producing diesel-engined buses and coaches, sixty-two of which were purchased by Irish operators, and then in 2018 it introduced fully electric passenger-carrying vehicles into its range. The first examples supplied to the UK and Irish market made their debut in 2020 and to date six have been sold in Eire and four to Big Lemon, Brighton.

Two years later, in 2021 UK van converter EVM launched an all-electric minibus, e-Cityline, which is based on the Mercedes-Benz Sprinter. A fifteen-seater, this is powered by three nickel manganese cobolt batteries, one of which is in the engine bay with the others beneath the floor, and the drive motor is mounted forward of the rear axle.

Promoted as the UK's first fully electric low-floor minibus was the Mellor Orion E, seen here as a demonstrator on a Fiat chassis in 2017. (Mellor)

The first operator to place an all-electric twenty-seven-seat Mellor Sigma 8 in service was Shuttle Buses, Kilwinning, who purchased two in December 2022, one of which, MX72HKZ, is seen here. (Author's collection)

The first English operator to purchase the electric Higer Steed was Big Lemon, Brighton, who bought four in 2022, one of which was twenty-seven-seat BIG949 which was new in June of that year. (John Law)

West Sussex minibus manufacturer EVM has added an electric version of its Cityline to its range, as seen here. (EVM)

Surprisingly, Mercedes-Benz has still yet to enter the UK bus market with a full-size electric bus, although it has announced that it intends to introduce its eCitaro (which made its debut in Europe in 2018) in 2022, so at the moment it is just a case of wait and see. Meanwhile, also waiting to make its debut is the Gamma Zero, built by Banbury-based Arrival UK, a new company set up in 2015 by Russian-born tech billionaire Denis Sverdlov with backing from some high-profile investors including Hyundai and Kia. Although only minimal details have so far been released, the all-electric Gamma Zero is a single-decker of a modular design/construction available in 10.5-metre and 12-metre lengths, has its batteries beneath the floor, is 40 per cent lighter than any of the other battery-electric buses currently on the market, and will optionally be AC or DC charged. Although it was understood that FirstGroup was to trial four examples in the autumn of 2021 and Edinburgh-based Ember had ordered four, before production of this new model began the company downsized its Banbury factory to concentrate on electric vans and has put the Gamma Zero on hold, and in February was placed into administration.

A further development making its debut was the fitting of solar panels to bus roofs, these providing the electricity to power a number of the vehicle's ancillaries as well as reduce fuel consumption and CO_2 emissions. Amongst the first UK users of these 3-mm thin, flexible solar roof panels are Go-Ahead South Coast (who have also fitted them to several of its MAN single-deckers in Singapore) and Stagecoach for its Oxford Tube vehicles, and if these prove successful it can be expected that other operators will ultimately follow suit.

In addition to electric vehicles are hydrogen fuel cell buses, which although relying on electrical power for propulsion, are not refuelled by plugging them into an EV charging station. The first trial with hydrogen power was undertaken in the late 1990s across the water in Chicago and Vancouver by New Flyer Industries and in the early 2000s Hino and Toyota began to develop hydrogen fuel cell technology and were steadily followed by others. The first buses using this form of power in the UK appeared in 2004 when Transport for London trialled three Mercedes-Benz Citaro single-deckers with roof-mounted hydrogen tanks. Although these were found to be successful, it was not until 2014 that any further hydrogen fuel cell buses appeared in Britain when ten tri-axle Van Hool A330s began operation in Aberdeen, followed in 2017 by a pair of conventional two-axle variants in London. Then, in November 2016, Wrightbus introduced the world's first hydrogen fuel cell double-decker, although the first were not placed in service until 2021 when they appeared in Aberdeen and were followed shortly afterwards with examples in London, Birmingham, and Dublin. Then, in 2019 Wrightbus introduced its integrally built GB Kite single-decker which could be powered by electricity (plug-in or pantograph charged) or hydrogen.

An artist's impression of the new triple-door Arrival Gamma Zero modular single-decker similar to those which were supposed to be trialled by FirstGroup. (Arrival)

This aerial view in 2016 of a line of buses in Hangzhou, China, shows that each is fitted with twenty roof-mounted solar panels. (Author's collection)

Seen here is a Go-Ahead Singapore diesel-engined MAN fitted with two roof-mounted solar panels similar to those on its UK South Coast buses. (Author's collection)

Supplied to First Capital in February 2011, hydrogen-powered VDL SB200 LK60HPL carries a Wrightbus dual-door body with seating for thirty-four passengers. (Wrightbus)

Purchased by Aberdeen City Council and pictured here when new in May 2014 is one of four hydrogen fuel cell-powered tri-axle Van Hool A330s operated on its behalf by First Aberdeen. (Van Hool)

Seen here when new, and before gaining its registration number, is Translink Metro's first hydrogen-powered Wrightbus StreetDeck. (Wrightbus)

Looking to the future, autonomous buses are now being developed which will allow their operation without drivers. One of the leaders in this form of transport is Aurrigo who in May 2021 introduced some ten-seat all-electric self-driving shuttles which will travel autonomously for most of the way on a 2-mile service from Madingley Road park & ride site to the University of Cambridge's West Campus. A year later, in conjunction with Solihull Council, Aurrigo began testing a similar shuttle connecting car park 5 with the terminal building at Birmingham Airport.

Following the above, in April 2022 Stagecoach, in partnership with Fusion Processing and Transport Scotland, began testing autonomous buses on a route from Ferrytoll park & ride across the River Forth to the Edinburgh Gateway train and tram interchange near the airport. Unlike the electric shuttles currently in use in Cambridge, Stagecoach used conventional-size diesel-powered Alexander Dennis E20D single-deckers manned by a safety driver. Despite the trials being successful, it was not until May2023 that the carriage of normal passengers on this 14-mile autonomous service began. Although autonomous buses were still in their infancy, driverless rail transport had first been introduced in the UK in August 1984 when a short, elevated, single-track driverless electronic shuttle was introduced by Maglev connecting Birmingham International rail station with the airport. Due to maintenance problems this closed in June 1995 but was ultimately replaced in 2003 with a driverless twin-track cable-hauled shuttle which is still operational today. Meanwhile, in August 1987 East London's Docklands Light Railway was inaugurated – built largely on closed railway lines and new concrete viaducts – and this was driverless and controlled by computers from a central point. With railed transport being easier to operate autonomously than vehicles using public roads, it is thus somewhat surprising that none of the UK's current tramway companies have yet moved towards a driverless system.

A further transport development was the combining of a tramway with the national rail system. In May 2018 South Yorkshire PTE, Stagecoach Supertram, and Northern Rail began trialling a service in conjunction with National Rail to operate trams conventionally from Sheffield to Meadowhall and then transferring them onto the national rail network to continue onwards to Rotherham and Parkgate Retail Park without the need to change from one mode of transport to another. Branded as Tramtrain, after finding this to be successful, passenger services commenced on 25 October of that same year and now annually attracts growing numbers of passengers.

Built by Aurrigo, Coventry, in May 2021 for Solihull MBC, ten-seat KX21GLV Autoshuttle is autonomously used at Brimingham Airport and the National Exhibition Centre. (Aurrigo)

New in 2018, this Navya Arma electrically powered autonomous shuttle bus was bought new in 2018 and placed in use in August 2022 by Inverness Campus and was operated on its behalf by Stagecoach. (Navya)

Stagecoach's autonomous ADL E20D 28326 (YX69NUH) was new in December 2019 as the project's demonstrator. (Stagecoach)

The original rail shuttle from Birmingham International rail station to the airport was, as seen here, operated with driverless Maglev cable cars. (Maglev)

Replacing the Maglev system were driverless cable-propelled twin cars built by Dopplemayr, these still being operational in 2024. (K. A. Jenkinson)

Seen at Docklands Light Railway Mudchute station on 3 June 2000 is one of its driverless four-coach trains. (K. A. Jenkinson)

Seen at Parkgate station in April 2019 is 399 206, one of Stagecoach Sheffield Supertram's tramtrains. (T. M. Leach collection)

With the environmental lobby continuing to grow and having gained much support from the government who at the end of March 2021 allocated a further £120 million funding for zero-emission buses, despite hybrid and diesel buses currently still at the moment being available on the UK market, it can perhaps be assumed that these will soon be phased out in favour of totally non-polluting vehicles. With electric buses having been available over a century ago, it proves that nothing is new, and has merely been refined. However, with hydrogen fuel cell technology appearing to be gaining momentum, particularly with Wrightbus treading this path due to its owner controlling hydrogen production company Ryse, it will be interesting to see if this will ultimately overtake battery-electric vehicles and leave history to repeat itself and again consign them to the past. Looking further into the future, experiments and developments are now being undertaken in liquid non-fossil fuels which could replace petrol and diesel without the need to ban these, and so for the moment it is a case of 'wait and see'.

Starting life as a demonstrator for its manufacturer in May 2018, hybrid-powered Wrightbus StreetDeck HEV SK18TKX was later purchased by Preston Bus. (Wrightbus)

Seen here before demonstration to Lothian Buses in March 2023 is MCV-bodied all-electric Volvo BZL BV23NNT with temporary fleet number 997. (Richard Walter)

Seen being displayed at the Bus & Coach Show at Birmingham's NEC in November 2022 is Irizar's new 12-metre dual-door all-electric ie-tram. (Author's collection)

New in February 2022 as a demonstrator, pure-electric Wrightbus Electroliner LY71GJE is seen here in Edinburgh being trialled by Lothian Buses. (Richard Walter)

On display at the NEC Bus & Coach Show in November 2022 is this 100 per cent electric midibus demonstrator built by Switch Mobility – previously called Optare. (Richard Walter)

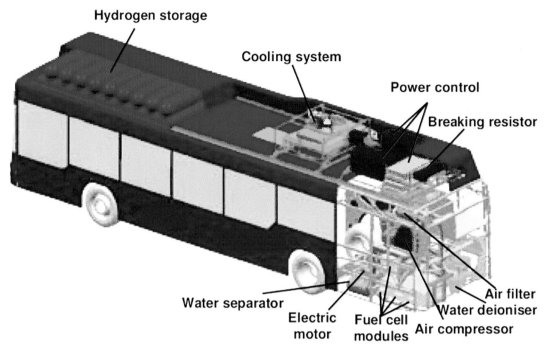

This diagram shows the position of all the components fitted to a hydrogen-powered bus.

Alexander Dennis's new hydrogen fuel cell-powered Enviro400FCEV, without any BYD input, is seen here in March 2023 before being given its registration number. (ADL)

Being evaluated by Lothian Buses is MCV-bodied all-electric Volvo BZL 997 (BV23NNT) which made its debut in March 2023. (Richard Walter)

Seen here undergoing a road trial is a new hybrid electric ADL Enviro400ER displaying 'Electric Range' branding and carrying fictitious registration YX69ADL. (ADL)

Unregistered when photographed on 25 April 2023, this all-electric Wrightbus GB Kite BEV was destined to join Translink Foyle Metro at Londonderry. (Paul Savage)

This photo of a Wrightbus GB Kite Hydroliner shows the tanks and other equipment mounted on the roof before the fitting of a second roof (cover) to complete the stylish design. (Wrightbus)